# What Wondrous Love

## Daily Prayers for *Lent* and *Holy Week* 2026

Written by Josh Noem

Ave Maria Press Notre Dame, Indiana

*Nihil Obstat:* Reverend Monsignor Michael Heintz, PhD
*Censor Librorum*
*Imprimatur:* Most Reverend Kevin C. Rhoades
Bishop of Fort Wayne–South Bend
Given at Fort Wayne, Indiana, on May 21, 2025

---



Founded in 1865, Ave Maria Press is a ministry of the United States Province of Holy Cross.

www.avemariapress.com

Paperback: ISBN-13 978-1-64680-421-4

E-book: ISBN-13 978-1-64680-422-1

Cover image © *Three Crosses Passion* by FaithArtCreation (faithartcreation.etsy.com). Used with permission.

Cover design by Samantha Watson.

Text design by Katherine Robinson.

Printed and bound in the United States of America.

# Introduction

We all know that prayer is the foundation of a life of faith—and that Lent is a time to intensify our focus on prayer—but that doesn't mean it is easy to do. This devotional is written for busy Catholics who are looking for a simple way to anchor their hearts and minds in God's presence every day throughout the Lenten season, from Ash Wednesday through Holy Week to Easter Sunday.

The season of Lent is a time to bring intentionality to our faith through the practices of prayer, fasting, and good works. These disciplines increase our capacity to receive the new life that Jesus has already won for us. Lent is also a time to journey with catechumens in our parishes who are in the final stages of preparing for Baptism at the Easter Vigil and others who will complete their initiation into the Church through Confirmation and/or the Eucharist. Walking with these individuals reminds us that faith makes a difference in the way we live—that our relationship with Jesus and his Church sets us apart and changes the trajectory of our lives.

Music engages our emotions; it lifts our hearts, as we acknowledge at every Mass. Each day of this devotional opens with a small portion of the lyrics from a well-known hymn—often from the gospel music tradition—that calls us to conversion. A short reflection on that text follows, along with prayers for morning and evening and a simple, spiritually focused question to think about throughout your day.

To help you pray, you can access a playlist of the songs featured in this book at www.avemariapress.com/pages/what-wondrous-love-music via your web browser or the QR codes that appear throughout this book (just focus your smartphone's camera on the QR code, and it will surface a link to the right page). Each song used here has three or four versions available for you to linger over and pray with as you listen. You can find the complete lyrics for each song beginning on page 50.

Lent is not a time to make ourselves holy—only God can do that. The effort and discipline we bring to our Lenten practice is our way of turning our lives over to God, stepping into the wondrous love of Jesus and following him to new and abundant life.

Ave Maria Press is a publishing ministry of the Congregation of Holy Cross, a religious order with a mission to educate in the faith by forming minds and hearts and drawing people into community. This book draws on the spirit that animates these priests and brothers—especially their motto: *Ave Crux, spes unica*, or "Hail the Cross, our only hope." Ave was founded more than 150 years ago to honor Mary, support the spiritual needs of our everyday living, and showcase the best of American Catholic writing.

Drawing on our Holy Cross heritage, Ave aims to set hearts on fire—and that's the aim and hope for this Lent and Holy Week devotional. Thank you for being part of our family of faith!

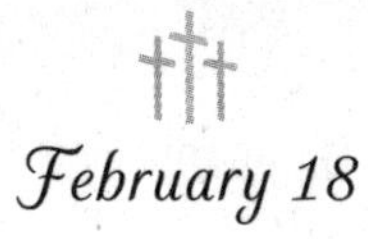

# February 18

## Ash Wednesday

Take up your cross, the Savior said,
if you would my disciple be.

Some of us have a detailed, robust program for the next forty days; some of us are just now thinking about where this Lenten season might take us. Either way, we begin our Lenten journey today with a sincere intention to follow Jesus more closely, knowing that his way leads us to the Cross.

We flock to the altar today to get ash smudged on our heads in the shape of a cross as a way to bear witness to this intention. Following Jesus means walking a path through suffering and sacrifice toward new life, just as he did. The ashes we wear also remind us of the urgency with which we seek transformation. We don't have unlimited time to grow in faithfulness. We will die one day, and our bodies will turn to dust. Now is the time to return to the Lord, to seek his mercy, and to ask for his strength.

### *Prayer for the Morning*

Jesus, Our Savior, you bore the Cross with courage and love. I know this Lenten journey will lead me to a confrontation with the crosses in my life—help me embrace them with hope. Jesus, Our Way, walk with me.

### *Ponder for the Day*

What are the crosses I am being asked to take up this Lent? What do I ask from Jesus to help me carry them?

### *Prayer for the Evening*

Jesus, Our Savior, you opened a way for us through death to eternal life. Intensify my urgency to seek and find you, and help me hold tightly to you in the weeks ahead. Jesus, Our Way, seek and find me.

*To listen to "Take Up Your Cross," scan the QR code or visit www.avemariapress.com/pages/what-wondrous-love-music.*

# *February 19*

## THURSDAY AFTER ASH WEDNESDAY

Deny yourself, the world forsake,
and humbly follow after me.

Our Lenten disciplines of prayer, fasting, and almsgiving are all rooted in the principle of self-denial. We would like to direct our time and attention, our desires, and our resources toward our own self-gratification, but we were created for more than this kind of self-centeredness. We've tried living by placing ourselves at the center, only to find there emptiness and dissatisfaction. We know we'll find purpose and meaning in our lives only if we center ourselves on love of God and neighbor—especially those who need it the most.

We step into this Lent boldly unafraid to deny ourselves because we know a joy and promise far greater than anything the world can give us.

### *Prayer for the Morning*

God of Love, you give us the world as though it were a garden to tend and grow—and in giving us yourself, you also provide us with so much more. Foster in me a desire for you that is stronger than my desire for self-satisfaction. God of Abundance, in you I have all I need.

### *Ponder for the Day*

What is the most difficult disposition or habit for me to let go of in my quest for self-denial? Why do I cling to this attachment?

### *Prayer for the Evening*

God of Love, you draw us to yourself through your Son, Jesus. Make me humble so that I can set aside my ways and follow him to you. God of Abundance, help me find you by letting go.

*To listen to "Take Up Your Cross," scan the QR code or visit*

# *February 20*

## Friday After Ash Wednesday

Take up your cross, which gives you strength,
which makes your trembling spirit brave.

What a strange thing to believe—that we can become strong by taking up and embracing that which makes us weak. How is this possible?

If we rely on our own strength, this is not possible—our spirits tremble. But Jesus suffered and died on the Cross—and then conquered death by his Resurrection. In him we make our way to union with God, even in the darkest moments. Nothing can stand in the way of the Father's love for us—not even death—if we but welcome friendship with Jesus and commit to following him. Our goal this Lent is to grow closer to Christ—because we need him. We can't do this life on our own.

### *Prayer for the Morning*

Lord of Life, you will enter any situation to seek us out and bring us to the Father. Find me in my weakness and help me trust your transformative love. Jesus, Our Brother, give me strength.

### *Ponder for the Day*

What makes my spirit tremble? How can I invite the Lord into this situation?

### *Prayer for the Evening*

Lord of Life, you willingly bore the Cross out of love for us—and you are near us in the crosses we carry. Help me face with honesty and courage the things that cause me grief and pain so that I might find you near me there. Jesus, Our Savior and Brother, make me brave.

*www.avemariapress.com/pages/what-wondrous-love-music.*

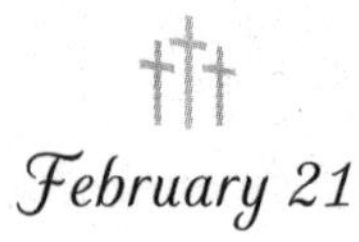

# *February 21*

## Saturday After Ash Wednesday

Take up your cross, be not ashamed! Let not disgrace your spirit fill!
For God himself endured to die upon a cross.

When we commit to facing our shortcomings and failings with honesty, we are confronted with shame. These feelings can become obstacles to our reaching for God because they can cause us to deem ourselves unworthy of God's love—a decision that is only God's to make.

Jesus embraced the Cross in order to prove to us that there is no end to God's love, no disgrace he will not endure to reach us. Many have tested the breadth and depth of his love and found no limit. God's boundless desire for us gives us confidence to reach for him despite our selfishness and imperfections; it also gives us courage to face those imperfections with clarity and sorrow for the ways they hold us back from loving as God does.

### *Prayer for the Morning*

Saving God, you stop at nothing to reach us. Help me to be honest about the ways I've fallen short of my dignity as your child and to trust that you love me—even when I don't love myself. Loving God, draw near to me.

### *Ponder for the Day*

What would change about my life if I reflected more of God's unconditional love?

### *Prayer for the Evening*

Saving God, you are merciful and forgiving and want nothing more than for us to return to you with burning hearts. Meet me in my desire for you, and refine and purify me so that I can more fully reflect your image. Loving God, transform me.

*To listen to "Take Up Your Cross" and "Forty Days and Forty Nights,"*

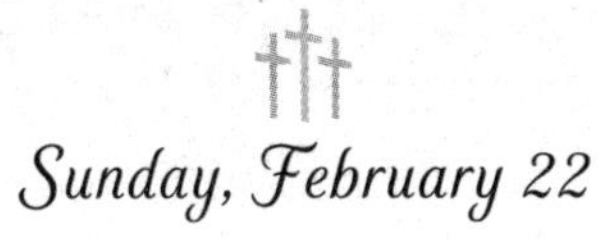

## *Sunday, February 22*

### First Week of Lent

Forty days and forty nights you were fasting in the wild . . .
tempted, and yet undefiled.

At Mass today, we hear about Jesus going into the desert and being tempted there. The forty days of our Lenten journey parallel the time he spends in the wilderness. But why did he go into the desert to fast in the first place? He could have fasted among friends and in the town where he was staying.

The wilderness provides clarity. There are no illusions, nothing to lean on. He's without shelter and protection. He's placing his life utterly in the Father's hands. And despite his weakness, this trust is what allows him to reject the temptations placed before him—he is honing his capacity to rely on God alone.

### *Prayer for the Morning*

Jesus, Son of God, you went into the desert to sharpen your faithfulness. Be with me as I set out on this forty-day journey to become more like you. Jesus, Faithful One, walk with me.

### *Ponder for the Day*

What parts of my life do I withhold from trusting God?

### *Prayer for the Evening*

Jesus, Son of God, you lived a life of complete trust in the Father. Deepen my faith so that I can follow you in placing my life in the hands of our Father. Jesus, Faithful One, lead me.

*scan the QR code or visit www.avemariapress.com/pages/what-wondrous-love-music.*

# *Monday, February 23*

## First Week of Lent

Shall not we your sorrow share, and from earthly joys abstain,
fasting with unceasing prayer, glad with you to suffer pain?

We don't embrace pain and suffering for their own sake, but they are unavoidable aspects of the human condition. During Lent, we take on the discipline of fasting and self-denial in order to grow our capacity to bear that suffering in a meaningful way, using it to unite ourselves with Jesus.

Prayer is the key that unlocks this door; spending time with the Lord every day, just as we are doing here now, unites our hearts to his. This is the transformation ahead of us this Lent: to invite God to strengthen, expand, and deepen our ability to make a gift of ourselves—even in the face of suffering.

### *Prayer for the Morning*

Jesus, Love of the Father, you walked into the desert to practice the discipline of self-denial knowing it was essential to your mission to reveal the fullness of God's love. Sustain me in my Lenten disciplines so that I may align more of my life with your self-giving way. Jesus, Love of My Life, enlarge my heart.

### *Ponder for the Day*

What small act of self-denial can I practice today in private in order to shrink my ego and expand my heart?

### *Prayer for the Evening*

Jesus, Love of the Father, you bore suffering with a humble heart. Fortify me with your Spirit so that I may grow closer to you through the sorrows I bear. Jesus, Love of My Life, draw me near.

*To listen to "Forty Days and Forty Nights," scan the QR code or visit*

## Tuesday, February 24

### First Week of Lent

And if Satan, vexing sore, flesh or spirit should assail,
Christ, his vanquisher before, grant we may not faint or fail.

Jesus shares every part of our humanity except for sin, which means that he knows what it's like to encounter temptation. He turned away from Satan's invitations in the desert and chose to rely upon God alone, which gave him the integrity and strength to remain true to who he is and to his mission.

His faithfulness lights a path for us when we, too, face temptation. We don't need to summon the willpower to turn away from Satan ourselves—we just have to turn to Jesus instead. Jesus vanquished the devil in the desert, Jesus vanquished him in his healing ministry, and Jesus vanquished him on the Cross. When Satan tempts us, Jesus will vanquish him for us as well.

### *Prayer for the Morning*

Christ, Our Savior, you came to restore us to our full dignity as daughters and sons of God. Guard me today and help me realize when I start to wander from your way so that I can return to you. Christ, the Power of God, lead me away from temptation.

### *Ponder for the Day*

We all have misplaced desires—how can I remember to run to Jesus when I'm feeling tempted?

### *Prayer for the Evening*

Christ, Our Savior, you are Lord of heaven and earth, and all creation bears witness to your truth, beauty, and goodness. Protect my heart and hold me close, safe in your love. Christ, the Power of God, deliver me from evil.

*www.avemariapress.com/pages/what-wondrous-love-music.*

# *Wednesday, February 25*

## First Week of Lent

Keep, oh, keep us, Savior dear, ever constant at your side;
that we may with you appear in your resurrection-tide.

In the first week of Lent, it's easy to invest our attention in prayer, fasting, and almsgiving that we want to embrace this season. But we should not lose sight of our destination—Easter. Lent expands our hearts so that we can enter more fully into the Death and Resurrection of Jesus.

We don't practice self-denial because we think we can save ourselves or earn our way to grace. We do it because it lessens our self-reliance, opens us to a deeper relationship with God and others, and makes us grateful and attentive—all of which bring us greater joy. This joy is the fruit of a life lived close to Christ because it is only in him that we approach what we were created for: love.

### *Prayer for the Morning*

Christ, Our Life, you are God's love for us in human form—the more we become like you, the more perfectly we are able to love God and neighbor. Remain with me and help me to make a gift of myself to further your kingdom. Christ, Our Joy, keep me by your side.

### *Ponder for the Day*

How might my Lenten disciplines bear fruit in joy today? How can I share that joy with someone else?

### *Prayer for the Evening*

Christ, Our Life, your Resurrection changed our destiny. Increase my longing to be united to you so that I may find in you fearlessness and abundant life. Christ, Our Joy, raise me up with you.

*To listen to "Forty Days and Forty Nights" and "Wayfaring Stranger,"*

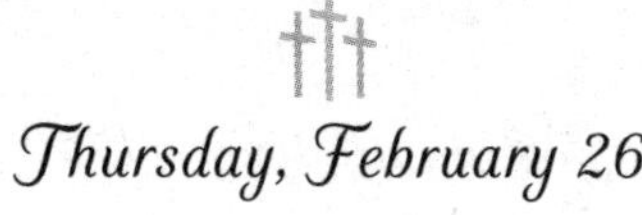

# Thursday, February 26

## First Week of Lent

I'm just a poor wayfaring stranger.

The forty days of Lent link us to our ancient ancestors in faith, the Israelites of the Old Testament, who wandered in the desert for forty years after Moses led them out of slavery in Egypt. They were a people on the move, longing for the Promised Land and learning to live in the in-between.

We live in a similar state of being in between: We live between this world and the next. We are a pilgrim people—wayfarers who are always restlessly searching for more. Lent reawakens that desire in us; the discomforts we take on as a discipline this season dislodge us from our comfort zones and keep us nimble and responsive to the new things God is doing in our lives.

The longing in the melody of this song reminds us that our restlessness is born from a deep desire that only God can satisfy, that we need to keep moving in search of God, and that we shouldn't get too comfortable.

### Prayer for the Morning

Eternal One, you are our source of peace. Keep my heart and mind anchored in your presence today so that I may find you wherever I go. God, Our Dwelling Place, abide in me today.

### Ponder for the Day

What is one area of my life where I'm perhaps too comfortable?

### Prayer for the Evening

Eternal One, you are our destiny, and you created us to live with you forever. Meet me in my restlessness and purify my desire so that I will seek you above all. God, Our Dwelling Place, call me home to you.

*scan the QR code or visit www.avemariapress.com/pages/what-wondrous-love-music.*

# *Friday, February 27*

## First Week of Lent

I'm just a going over Jordan,
I'm just a going over home.

After the Israelites had wandered in the desert for forty years, they finally crossed over the River Jordan and entered the Promised Land, a land of abundance. As a pilgrim people, we, too, long for a place of abundance and peace where we will be one with God and all our desires will be fulfilled. That place will be heaven when we die, but we get glimpses of that fullness in the here and now when God's kingdom breaks into our experience.

In our day-to-day living, we start to wander; we forget that we have a destination and begin to follow lesser desires. Lent is a time to reorient ourselves—to point our hearts back to God, our source and end, our one true home. Lent is a time to recall that we ought not to wander through life; we are meant to walk with purpose.

### *Prayer for the Morning*

Spirit of Grace and Prayer, you led the Israelites over the River Jordan to the Promised Land. Help me follow your promptings today so that I may live in the abundance of the Father. Gift of God, lead me in the way of salvation.

### *Ponder for the Day*

What habits have I picked up during this past year that cause me to wander from God? How can I reorient myself?

### *Prayer for the Evening*

Spirit of Grace and Prayer, you reach into our lives to draw us into communion. Teach me to pray in a way that deepens my union with the Trinity. Gift of God, breathe your life into me.

*To listen to "Wayfaring Stranger," scan the QR code or visit*

## *Saturday, February 28*

### First Week of Lent

I'm going there to see my loved ones,
they passed before me one by one.

We are on the move toward heaven, where we will be united with God and all those who have gone before us. This passage to paradise is made possible by Jesus, who created a way for us through his Cross, Death, and Resurrection. Our participation in this Paschal Mystery allows us to find and receive God's mercy, no matter how distant we feel from him. Our faithfulness allows us to follow Jesus's way through the Cross to new and abundant life.

What we do in this life has eternal consequences. This Lent, let us do what we can to get our lives in order so that we can practice in this world the loving union and pure hearts we hope for in the next.

### *Prayer for the Morning*

God, the Father of Heaven, you created us for communion. Guide me in your way of love today. Father of Love, holy is your name.

### *Ponder for the Day*

Call to mind loved ones who have died, and ask for their intercession for your Lenten journey.

### *Prayer for the Evening*

God, the Father of Heaven, all of creation finds fullness of being in you. Re-create me in your image, and make me a sign of your loving presence for others. Father of Love, may your kingdom come.

*www.avemariapress.com/pages/what-wondrous-love-music.*

## Sunday, March 1

### Second Week of Lent

Beautiful Savior, King of Creation, Son of God and Son of Man!

In this second week of Lent, we turn our attention to the Transfiguration (Mt 17:1–9), when Jesus's divinity bursts forth atop Mt. Tabor. It's an odd event to ponder in this season of repentance. Why is the Church connecting this moment in Jesus's life with Lent?

Ten days into our Lenten journey, our initial Ash Wednesday enthusiasm has started to wear thin—but we're only a quarter of the way to Easter. So maybe we could use some encouragement just about now.

Jesus is both Son of God and Son of Man who became one of us so that we could become like God. The gospels help us imagine his humanity, but his divinity shines forth in the Transfiguration. This moment of glory reveals our own destiny—if we follow him to the Cross. Let us persevere in our Lenten commitments with hope that they will make us more like Jesus.

### *Prayer for the Morning*

King of Creation, you are both fully divine and fully human. Open my eyes and heart to see the ways you are breaking forth into my experience today. Beautiful Savior, shine in my life with your glory.

### *Ponder for the Day*

Recall the last "mountaintop experience" you had in your life of faith. What part of that memory can you carry with you today?

### *Prayer for the Evening*

King of Creation, as your brothers and sisters, we share your mission to establish God's kingdom in the here and now. Transform me so that my love might reveal God's glory. Beautiful Savior, let your glory shine through me.

*To listen to "Beautiful Savior," scan the QR code or visit*

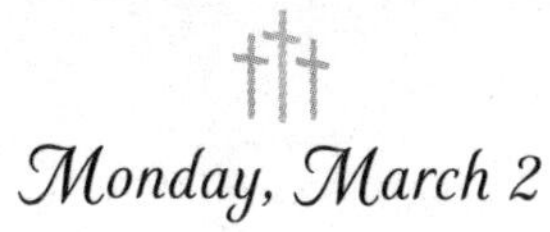

# *Monday, March 2*

## Second Week of Lent

Robed in flow'rs of blooming spring;
Jesus is fairer, Jesus is purer; he makes our sorr'wing spirit sing.

The term *Lent* comes from Old English and German terms for spring, and it's no accident that this is the season of the year we set aside for renewal. New life is sprouting all around us as the days lengthen and warm. In northern areas, color returns as the gray winter gives way to green buds and flowers. In her wisdom, the Church uses this season as a sign and symbol of what Jesus accomplishes in us. The warmth and energy of his love melt away what was dark and cold in our hearts and awaken new life there.

We are making intentional changes in the way we live so that we more closely imitate Jesus. As we enter more deeply into his love for us, we experience sorrow for the ways we've selfishly turned away from him. Yet we also know hope because we know he is rich in mercy. Our spirits sing.

### *Prayer for the Morning*

Merciful Savior, you walk with us in the concrete circumstances of our daily living. Awaken me to your nearness and help me grow in your love. Jesus, Our Life, renew me.

### *Ponder for the Day*

What parts of my life are cold and gray? Where do I most need the warmth of Jesus's love?

### *Prayer for the Evening*

Merciful Savior, you appear to us fair and pure, robed in flowers. Make me bloom with your new life and clothe me with your beauty. Jesus, Our Life, make my spirit sing.

*www.avemariapress.com/pages/what-wondrous-love-music.*

# *Tuesday, March 3*

## Second Week of Lent

Jesus shines brighter, Jesus shines purer
than all the angels in the sky.

One of the brilliant details of the Bible story of the Transfiguration is the way Jesus's "face shone like the sun and his clothes became white as light" (Mt 17:2). Peter, James, and John talked about this wonder with the other disciples, then this detail was handed down in spoken word, and, finally, it was written into the gospels of Matthew, Mark, and Luke. The disciples perceived Jesus's divine nature as a revelation of near-blinding light.

Christ's light guides our path over these forty days of Lent. Turning away from our selfish desires and turning toward Jesus is like turning to the sun: His truth enlightens our way, his goodness brings us nourishing energy, and his beauty warms us.

### *Prayer for the Morning*

Jesus, Dayspring from on High, your love is a light for our way. Illuminate my Lenten journey so that I may see more clearly the way to follow you today. Christ, Our Light, burn in me.

### *Ponder for the Day*

How might I bring some of Christ's light to others today?

### *Prayer for the Evening*

Jesus, Dayspring from on High, your relentless love is a consuming fire. Burn away anything within me that is not true, good, or beautiful. Christ, Our Light, purify me.

*To listen to "Beautiful Savior" and "Blessed Assurance," scan the QR*

# *Wednesday, March 4*

## Second Week of Lent

Heir of Salvation, Purchase of God,
born of his Spirit, washed in his blood.

Cradle Catholics are familiar with the rhythms of Lent: the prayer, fasting, and almsgiving disciplines that put into our bodies and hearts the conversion we know we need. Because we've been doing this our whole lives, we draw near to our catechumens, who are moving through Lent as a final stage of a drastic reorientation of their lives. These converts have come to believe that being baptized into the mystery of Jesus's Death and Resurrection makes us adopted children of God. And they are ready to publicly profess that faith and live by it. We walk with these catechumens in this season and hold them close in prayer because we need the witness of their lives—they remind us that this faith matters and is worth giving our lives to.

### *Prayer for the Morning*

Savior, through our Baptism we are washed in your blood and born of your Spirit. Grant me urgency and single-heartedness in my Lenten return to you. Jesus, Our Brother, save me.

### *Ponder for the Day*

Spend time today praying for the catechumens preparing for Baptism and their confession of faith. Ask your Confirmation saint for their intercession as well!

### *Prayer for the Evening*

Savior, your Death and Resurrection changed our destiny and restored us to God. Re-create me in your divine image. Jesus, Our Brother, renew me.

*code or visit www.avemariapress.com/pages/what-wondrous-love-music.*

# *Thursday, March 5*

## Second Week of Lent

This is my story, this is my song,
praising my Savior all the day long.

When we are right with ourselves, with God, and with the world, we see ourselves in proper perspective: We are creatures of a God who loved us into being and constantly reaches out to bring us into deeper union with himself. This right vision of the world inspires in us gratitude and wonder, which overflow into praise of God. When we praise God, we stand firmly in our role as his beloved children. God does not need our praise and worship; we offer him our thanks because it is the only thing we can offer in response to all he gives us. With this hymn today, we claim this rightly ordered praise as the defining story of our lives—as our story and our song.

### *Prayer for the Morning*

Heavenly Father, you made us out of love, and you hold every moment of our lives with intimate care. Deepen my gratitude for the wonderful gift of being your beloved. Loving Creator, I sing your praise.

### *Ponder for the Day*

Spend a moment in the middle of your day today delighting in the wonder of existence—breathing deeply and thanking God for the gift of life and his love for you.

### *Prayer for the Evening*

Heavenly Father, our story turns into a song when it conforms to the Truth, who is your Son come to share in our humanity. Tune my life and bring me into harmony with your eternal, loving design. Loving Creator, make me true.

*To listen to "Blessed Assurance," scan the QR code or visit*

# Friday, March 6

## Second Week of Lent

Perfect submission, all is at rest.
I in my Savior am happy and bless'd.

As people of faith, we know the insufficiency of living according to our own designs and ends and the damage this causes to our relationships. When we live for ourselves, we become subject to the tyranny of our own desires and impose our will on others. In this season of repentance, we are trying to turn away from this selfishness because we know it's fruitless.

Faith orients us toward love, which is another name for God. Because we were created for self-gift, love leads us to joy and new life. The goal of our Lenten practice is to love more perfectly, to practice in a small but intentional way the kind of selflessness that Jesus embodied on the Cross because it is a path to abundant life. This is the paradox of faith: By letting go, we find rest; by submitting to God's designs, we find freedom; by giving ourselves away, we find ourselves; and by dying, we live.

### *Prayer for the Morning*

God of Freedom, you sent your Son as the definitive revelation of your love for us. Grant me the courage and clarity to follow his way of selflessness more perfectly. God of Love, increase my faith.

### *Ponder for the Day*

When do I feel restless? What is the deeper truth God is inviting me to embrace in those situations?

### *Prayer for the Evening*

God of Freedom, you created us in your image. Help me live in obedience to your designs so that I may find rest in you. God of Love, increase my joy.

*www.avemariapress.com/pages/what-wondrous-love-music.*

# *Saturday, March 7*

## Second Week of Lent

Filled with his goodness, lost in his love.

The author of these lyrics, Fanny Crosby, wrote more than eight thousand hymns. Known as the "queen of gospel song writers," she was a household name in the early 1900s. She was born blind and memorized most of the Bible; she credits this rich interior life as the source of her compositional creativity. "If perfect earthly sight were offered me tomorrow, I would not accept it," she once said. "I might not have sung hymns to the praise of God if I had been distracted by the beautiful and interesting things about me."

Faith was interwoven in Crosby's life as deeply as her own heartbeat—it was simply the air she breathed. That intimacy with God bore fruit in song and lyrical writing that continues to form us. Our task this Lent is to clear space in our lives for God to deepen our faith, strengthen our hope, and embolden our love so that our lives may also bear great fruit.

### *Prayer for the Morning*

Loving Savior, you are the source of everything that is true, good, and beautiful. Grant me the interior awareness to recognize your presence with me today. Jesus, fill me with your goodness.

### *Ponder for the Day*

What is one selfless act I can offer someone today as a way for my faith to bear fruit in the world?

### *Prayer for the Evening*

Loving Savior, you invite us to join you in establishing God's kingdom in the here and now. Let your love fill and flow through me to touch the people you have placed in my life. Jesus, make my life a song.

*To listen to "Blessed Assurance" and "Softly and Tenderly Jesus*

# *Sunday, March 8*

## Third Week of Lent

Softly and tenderly Jesus is calling, calling for you and for me;
see, on the portals he's waiting and watching, watching for you and for me.

In this third week of Lent, the Church invites us to contemplate the encounter between Jesus and the woman at the well (Jn 4). When he passed through Samaria, Jesus stopped at a well and met a woman there. The exchange that followed changed her life.

Besides all of the norms Jesus was breaking during that encounter—a Jewish man addressing a Samaritan woman—the first detail to notice was that he *waited* for her. He was tired, hot, and thirsty. He could have been somewhere comfortable, resting from his journey. Instead, he placed himself at a busy intersection and waited to see whom he'd find there.

Jesus is watching and waiting for us this Lent as well, ready to encounter us and change our lives with his living water.

### *Prayer for the Morning*

Jesus, Fountain of Living Water, you sought out the Samaritan woman because you knew she was looking for new life. Be patient with me in my search for you—help me find you today. Jesus, Divine Healer, wait for me.

### *Ponder for the Day*

Who might God put in your life today with an opportunity for a meaningful conversation? How can you watch and wait for that encounter?

### *Prayer for the Evening*

Jesus, Fountain of Living Water, your words bring life. Open my ears and heart to hear when you call, and strengthen my will to respond to you. Jesus, Divine Healer, watch for me.

*Is Calling," scan the QR code or visit www.avemariapress.com/pages/what-wondrous-love-music.*

## *Monday, March 9*

### Third Week of Lent

Earnestly, tenderly, Jesus is calling,
calling, O sinner, come home!

Home is the place where we belong, where we are known through and through, where we are loved. Home could be the place where our family raised us; it might also be something we create for ourselves in other circumstances. Either way, when we're in the space we know as home, we are fully ourselves—we have confidence we'll find there the safety and nourishment we need to thrive.

Lent is a time to grow in our awareness of how our selfishness has set us out wandering in search of love and acceptance and comfort in places other than in God. This is a time to come home to the one place where we truly find ourselves. Moments of prayer and reflection, like this one we're in right now, attune our ears to the Lord calling us back to deeper communion.

### *Prayer for the Morning*

God, Our Help, you created us to know and love you. Deepen my desire for you so that I may hear your voice when I am restless and in need of comfort. God, Our Strength, call me home.

### *Ponder for the Day*

How do I tend to wander from God? What am I really seeking?

### *Prayer for the Evening*

God, Our Help, we find our rest only in you. Call to me when I stray and return me to myself, where I am grounded in your endless love. God, Our Strength, bring me home.

*To listen to "Softly and Tenderly Jesus Is Calling," scan the QR code*

# *Tuesday, March 10*

## Third Week of Lent

Time is now fleeting, the moments are passing, passing from you and from me;
shadows are gathering, deathbeds are coming, coming for you and for me.

Though the ashes we received at the start of Lent have long been washed away, we are still called to the urgency they represent. We don't have unlimited time on this earth. We are dust and to dust we shall return. We will come face-to-face with our Maker when the great gift of this life is through.

But we've received an even greater gift: We've been adopted as children of a God who loves us and who reaches into history—into the specific circumstances of the lives of each one of us—to save us.

The urgency we feel is not a sense that we have to hurry to make ourselves right before we die. We've already been saved; we are already loved into eternity. The urgency we feel is to not waste a moment diving deeper into this love to be more fully transformed by it.

### *Prayer for the Morning*

God, Our Refuge, you are love—you extend to us the gift of yourself without condition. Help me perceive the magnitude of this gift and to reflect your generosity in my life today. Rock of Salvation, hold me close.

### *Ponder for the Day*

Spend time today praying for loved ones who have preceded you in death.

### *Prayer for the Evening*

God, Our Refuge, you offer yourself to us freely and without reservation in an unending gift—there is nothing we can do to earn or become unworthy of your love. Plunge me ever deeper into your intimate care for me and let me shine with your selfless glory. Rock of Salvation, embrace me.

*or visit www.avemariapress.com/pages/what-wondrous-love-music.*

# *Wednesday, March 11*

## Third Week of Lent

O for the wonderful love he has promised, promised for you and for me!
Though we have sinned, he has mercy and pardon, pardon for you and for me.

One of the first fruits of deepening prayer is the awareness of our sinfulness. When we encounter the depth of God's love for us, we realize how often we fall short of that gift. The shame and guilt we feel are natural responses that spur us to change our lives.

Sometimes remorse can become an obstacle to our return, however. We balk at surfacing guilt because it threatens our self-esteem and makes us feel unworthy of God's love. But one of the wonders and mysteries of our faith is the hope and promise that Jesus came and died for us *knowing that we would reject him*. It is precisely because we feel unworthy of his love that he reaches out to us. The more distant we feel from God, the more of a claim he lets us have on his mercy.

### *Prayer for the Morning*

God of Endless Mercy, you will let nothing come in the way of our return to you. Deepen my trust in your love for me, especially when I feel far from it. Loving Father, reach for me.

### *Ponder for the Day*

What are the parts of my life that bring me shame and guilt? How can I place those feelings before God today?

### *Prayer for the Evening*

God of Endless Mercy, you sent your Son to take on the burden of our guilt. Help me confront my sin with honesty and truthfulness, knowing that your love is stronger than death. Loving Father, I reach for you.

*To listen to "Softly and Tenderly Jesus Is Calling" and "There's a*

# *Thursday, March 12*

## Third Week of Lent

There's a wideness in God's mercy,
like the wideness of the sea.

The sea is beyond what we can imagine. We can picture the blue areas painted on a globe in a library, but stand on the sand of a beach facing west from Oregon with wet, salty wind pelting your face and the drumming beat of rolling waves endlessly pushing foam at your feet, and you can't imagine how much water is out there. You know intellectually that Japan is beyond the horizon, but the mind can't grasp the volume of water in between. We can imagine *parts* of the ocean—the blue of the Caribbean, the ice floes of the Arctic, the swells of the Pacific, the warmth of the Gulf, and the white chop on the slate blue of the Atlantic—but the whole is too big to truly comprehend.

And God's mercy is bigger than all that.

### *Prayer for the Morning*

Eternal One, you are immeasurable love. Expand my heart and imagination to receive more of what you want to give me, and help me conform my life according to the magnitude of this gift. God of Mercy, I wade into you.

### *Ponder for the Day*

How would your prayer change if you imagined approaching God in the way you experience the ocean?

### *Prayer for the Evening*

Eternal One, you created us in your self-giving image. Mold my heart to your generosity so that I may pour out your love through the service I offer others. God of Mercy, immerse me.

*Wideness in God's Mercy," scan the QR code or visit www.avemariapress.com/pages/what-wondrous-love-music.*

# *Friday, March 13*

## Third Week of Lent

There is mercy with the Savior, there is healing in his blood.

How do we know God is merciful and trust his love reigns supreme?

God told us exactly what he is like—he sent his Son to us to reveal everything we need to know about him. Though human beings rejected his Son—*killed* him—God didn't scorch the earth in fury. Instead, he turned that violence into nourishment. He turned our evil into an even greater good by using it to conquer death.

Jesus came to reveal to us the depth and breadth of God's love. We spilled his blood, and he uses it to heal us. We lifted him upon a cross, and he transforms it into a sign of hope. We killed him, and he gives us eternal life. This is the mystery of love that we seek to enter into and be transformed by this Lent.

### *Prayer for the Morning*

Jesus, Indescribable Gift of the Father, your Death and Resurrection opened the gates of heaven to us. Form me in the mystery of your love so that I may have eternal life. Christ, Our Hope of Salvation, have mercy on me.

### *Ponder for the Day*

How might I change my approach to a grievance or grudge in my life by reflecting more of the undeserved and unconditional love Jesus has for us?

### *Prayer for the Evening*

Jesus, Indescribable Gift of the Father, through our Baptism, we have been adopted into God's family and made members of your Body in the world. Immerse me in the life of your Church, where I might find your transforming grace. Christ, Our Hope of Salvation, heal me.

*To listen to "There's a Wideness in God's Mercy," scan the QR code or*

# *Saturday, March 14*

## Third Week of Lent

If our love were but more simple, we should rest upon God's word,
and our lives would be illumined by the presence of our Lord.

When Jesus met the woman at the well, he didn't offer her an easy life. She believed he was who he said he was, but her troubles were not magically erased. Rather, his revelation of God's love to her was an invitation to participate in it. She went into the community with fearlessness to proclaim it, and, as John's gospel tells us, "Many of the Samaritans of that town began to believe in him because of the word of the woman who testified" (4:39). She showed up at the well seeking water for her thirst; she left transformed into a well of living water for others who thirsted for good news.

Our hymn for the second part of this week reminds us of God's mercy, encouraging us to trust it—not because it will make our lives easy but because it will make us more like his Son.

### *Prayer for the Morning*

Jesus, Word of Life, you are the Anointed One, the Messiah sent to establish God's kingdom. Make my love simple so that I may participate in your reign. Jesus, the Way, shine in my life.

### *Ponder for the Day*

Whom will God place in your life today with an opportunity to reveal his mercy?

### *Prayer for the Evening*

Jesus, Word of Life, your presence is a light for our path. In all my seeking after holiness this Lent, let me not forget that you are already near. Jesus, the Way, I rest in you.

*visit www.avemariapress.com/pages/what-wondrous-love-music.*

## *Sunday, March 15*

### Fourth Week of Lent

I am bound for the promised land; oh, who will come and go with me?

Like the Israelites who journeyed through the desert for forty years, we are people on the way. We are restless until we find our home in the promised land of heaven. Our Lenten journey is only a few weeks long, but that is enough to dislodge us from our comfort zones. Our prayer, fasting, and almsgiving keep us on our toes, responsive to the promptings of love.

The melody of today's hymn, "On Jordan's Stormy Banks I Stand," carries both longing and joy, which are good dispositions to travel with in this season. Some renditions present this chorus in a round with a call-and-response echo, reminding us that we do not travel alone. Together, we proclaim our destination—the promised land of communion with God and his People—and we travel with resolve, gathering fellow pilgrims all along the way.

### *Prayer for the Morning*

Eternal Spirit, you form us as God's People and spur us to keep moving toward deeper union. Guard me from settling into self-centeredness and spur me toward intimacy with the Father. Spirit of Glory, keep me moving.

### *Ponder for the Day*

In what ways could my life be too comfortable—and where might God be calling me to go?

### *Prayer for the Evening*

Eternal Spirit, you inflame our hearts with your love. Increase my desire for heaven so that I may recognize the surprising ways God's kingdom breaks through in the here and now. Spirit of Glory, move in me.

*To listen to "On Jordan's Stormy Banks I Stand," scan the QR code or*

# *Monday, March 16*

## Fourth Week of Lent

When I shall reach that happy place, I'll be forever blest,
for I shall see my Father's face, and in his bosom rest.

God wants one thing of us: love. And because he is Love, we grow closer to him when we love others, especially when we share ourselves with those who feel distant from God because of wounds or injustice or poverty or violence. Our prayer, fasting, and almsgiving this Lent are not an exercise in self-transcendence or reaching for enlightenment—instead of elevating ourselves, our disciplines help us *empty* ourselves.

If we long for "that happy place" where we will rest in the Father, we have an opportunity to create such a place here in this life by letting the love we receive overflow in service to our neighbors in need. We don't have to wait for heaven to see God's face.

### *Prayer for the Morning*

Jesus, Consolation of the Father, you showed preferential care to those on the margins. Expand my heart to include those who suffer in forgotten ways so that I may be a sign of your love and receive from them your friendship. Christ, Our Brother, strengthen me.

### *Ponder for the Day*

Who is someone living near me—in my neighborhood or community—in need of God's consolation?

### *Prayer for the Evening*

Jesus, Consolation of the Father, you are love incarnate. Grant me the courage and compassion to speak your Word to those searching for hope. Christ, Our Brother, send me.

*visit www.avemariapress.com/pages/what-wondrous-love-music.*

# *Tuesday, March 17*

## Memorial of St. Patrick

Christ be in my heart and mind,
Christ within my soul enshrined.

The lyrics of our song for today are taken from a *lorica*, a type of prayer from the Middle Ages. Originally, a lorica was the name for the upper-body metal armor worn by Roman soldiers, so naturally, as a prayer, a lorica asks for protection.

This lorica is attributed to St. Patrick, whose feast we celebrate today (it's sometimes referred to as the prayer of his breastplate). Through a litany, he invites Christ into every dimension of life: "around, above, below" as a shield against evil. We follow Patrick today and invoke the presence of Christ to accompany us in every direction, especially in our hearts and minds, so that we may enshrine him in our soul at every moment.

### *Prayer for the Morning*

Christ, My Life and Only Way, you came into this world to share in every aspect of our humanity. I invite you into every aspect of my day. Christ, My Unchanging Friend, I arise today through your mighty strength.

### *Ponder for the Day*

How can I carry Christ with me today so that he may appear in every heart that thinks of me?

### *Prayer for the Evening*

Christ, My Life and Only Way, nothing is more powerful than your love for us. Protect me from the snares of wickedness and the seduction of vices. Christ, My Unchanging Friend, secure and shelter me.

*To listen to "Christ Be Near at Either Hand" and "The King of Love*

# *Wednesday, March 18*

## Fourth Week of Lent

The King of Love my shepherd is, whose goodness fails me never.
I nothing lack if I am his, and he is mine forever.

Today's hymn, "The King of Love My Shepherd Is," unfolds in four phrases. The first two repeat a pattern, and the third soars over the top of them before the fourth resolves the arc. What a remarkable line! "I nothing lack if I am his," and it's delivered with a melody that makes us feel expansive and abundant. The composition here allows us to feel what we're praying. If you've ever had the chance to sing this as part of a congregation, it's easy to belt out.

God created the world out of his own goodness; as a union of love, the Trinity didn't need any of the universe in which we live. But love is self-gift, so this dappled creation sprang from the inner life of their communion. We have the power of this creative love burning within each one of us. What else could we possibly need?

### *Prayer for the Morning*

Jesus, your goodness fails us never. As I seek to follow your self-giving way, deepen my trust that you will provide all I need. King of Love, I am yours.

### *Ponder for the Day*

How can I stoke the flame of the creative love of the Trinity within me—and what good works will it ignite in me today?

### *Prayer for the Evening*

Jesus, we lack nothing when we are united with you. Shepherd me to align my life with your will and design so that I may live in your abundance. King of Love, you are mine.

*My Shepherd Is," scan the QR code or visit www.avemariapress.com/pages/what-wondrous-love-music.*

# *Thursday, March 19*

## Solemnity of St. Joseph

Where streams of living water flow, my ransomed soul he leadeth;
and where the verdant pastures grow, with food celestial feedeth.

We celebrate the faithfulness of St. Joseph today. God spoke to him in dreams, and Joseph's decision to listen to God's voice allowed him to create a family. This was a man of action who trusted God to lead him.

When he was prompted to flee their home with Mary to protect the newborn Jesus, Joseph likely didn't feel they were being led to streams of living water—as refugees, they probably didn't find Egypt to be a verdant pasture. But he trusted that God would care for them like a good shepherd—he knew that God would keep them safe and provide what they needed. So he faithfully followed.

### *Prayer for the Morning*

St. Joseph, Protector of the Holy Family and the Church, you were attuned to God's voice in prayer and trusted where it led you. Pray for me so that I may also hear God speaking and have the courage to act. Joseph Most Faithful, help me listen and follow.

### *Ponder for the Day*

How is God leading you in a new and unexpected direction at this point in your life? What is the next step in following his prompting?

### *Prayer for the Evening*

St. Joseph, Protector of the Holy Family and the Church, in following the promptings of the Spirit, you became more like our Father in heaven. Help me place my life in God's hands as well so that I may reflect his love to those he's placed in my life. Joseph Most Faithful, help me trust.

*To listen to "The King of Love My Shepherd Is," scan the QR code or*

# *Friday, March 20*

## Fourth Week of Lent

In death's dark vale I fear no ill, with thee, dear Lord, beside me;
thy rod and staff my comfort still, thy cross before to guide me.

This hymn draws from the images we receive in Psalm 23, one of the most famous passages in the Bible. There's a reason it's so well known: It presents with clarity the fundamental challenge of faith, which is to place our lives in God's hands with trust that God will give us what we need. Even when we face the darkness of death, we don't need to fear because God has made a way for us through the Death and Resurrection of his Son.

As we approach Holy Week, our Lenten observance becomes even more urgent and important because we want to enter the mystery of Jesus's saving love with all we are. We place the Cross before us as a sign of our hope, ready to follow Jesus through death's dark vale.

### *Prayer for the Morning*

Good Shepherd, you care for our every need and stand ready to provide for as much as we entrust to you. Grant me courage and trust to rely on you. Dear Lord, comfort and guide me.

### *Ponder for the Day*

What are the small ways I'll encounter the Cross today, and how can I look to Christ in those moments to guide me?

### *Prayer for the Evening*

Good Shepherd, you entered our human condition in every way but sin, accepting even humiliation, suffering, and death. Deepen my faith that you remain near me, ready to guide me in your life-giving ways. Dear Lord, stay beside me.

*visit www.avemariapress.com/pages/what-wondrous-love-music.*

## *Saturday, March 21*

### Fourth Week of Lent

Perverse and foolish, oft I strayed, but yet in love he sought me;
and on his shoulder gently laid, and home, rejoicing, brought me.

The author of this hymn was a pastor in England named Henry Williams Baker. He died in 1877 at the age of fifty-five, and on his deathbed, he recited this verse. Of all the many hymns he wrote, these were the lyrics that he clung to as he passed from this life.

Knowing that he would soon meet his Creator, Baker held fast to the belief that despite his waywardness, Jesus would seek him out and carry him home. Jesus tells us plainly that he does the same for us—just read the tenth chapter of John's gospel. There Jesus tells us, "I am the good shepherd. A good shepherd lays down his life for the sheep" (10:11).

Like Baker, we can take courage this Lent, especially if we've strayed. Jesus seeks us nonetheless, and rejoices when he finds us.

### *Prayer for the Morning*

Jesus, Our Leader and Savior, you are the Good Shepherd who knows his sheep. Help me remember that, even when I wander, you are near, ready to welcome me home. Jesus, Guardian of Our Souls, bring me home rejoicing.

### *Ponder for the Day*

How have I strayed this Lent? How have I experienced Jesus seeking me?

### *Prayer for the Evening*

Jesus, Our Leader and Savior, you came so that we could have life abundantly. Grant me courage so that I may persevere in faithfulness. Jesus, Guardian of Our Souls, seek me out in love.

*To listen to "The King of Love My Shepherd Is" and "Where We'll*

# *Sunday, March 22*

## Fifth Week of Lent

There we never shall die,
'tis a land where we never grow old.

As we draw near to Holy Week, we hear the account of Jesus's raising of Lazarus. Though he lived to die again, the miracle Jesus worked for Lazarus demonstrates his power over life and death. As Jesus told the grieving Martha, "I am the resurrection and the life; whoever believes in me, even if he dies, will live, and everyone who lives and believes in me will never die. Do you believe this?" (Jn 11:25–26).

He asks us this question as well. We participate in Jesus's life to the extent that we participate in his self-giving love. Our task in the remaining days of this Lent is to intensify our selflessness so that when we reach Easter, we can joyously rise with Jesus from the tomb of sin and sorrow into new and glorious life.

### *Prayer for the Morning*

Jesus, the Resurrection, you will an abundance of divine life for us. Increase my capacity for selflessness as I strive to follow your way. Jesus, Our Life, raise me up.

### *Ponder for the Day*

What is the tomb that Jesus is calling you out of this Lent?

### *Prayer for the Evening*

Jesus, the Resurrection, you called Lazarus from the grave and promise the same for us when you come again in glory. Increase my faith and hope in you as my source of life. Jesus, triumph in me.

*Never Grow Old," scan the QR code or visit www.avemariapress.com/pages/what-wondrous-love-music.*

# *Monday, March 23*

## Fifth Week of Lent

In that beautiful home where we'll nevermore roam,
we shall be in the sweet by and by.

Jesus comes to bring us closer into perfect union with the Father. "I am the way and the truth and the life," he says. "No one comes to the Father except through me" (Jn 14:6).

Our hymn for today and tomorrow, "Where We'll Never Grow Old," imagines this intimacy as a "beautiful home," a place where we can dwell together. We often think of this communion as our final destination in heaven, but it is also a place inside of us now. By encountering the living God through his Spirit moving within us—an encounter that is available to us in every moment, including now—we find our true home. When we are with God we don't need to roam, because we have found our heart's desire.

### *Prayer for the Morning*

Jesus, Our Truth, you draw us ever deeper into the mystery of the love of the Trinity. Increase my love and my longing for you. Jesus, Our Life, dwell in me.

### *Ponder for the Day*

No matter where this day takes me, how can I remain in my "beautiful home" with the Father?

### *Prayer for the Evening*

Jesus, Our Truth, you prepare a place for us in your Father's house. Meet me as I seek your presence in my prayer and bring me home. Jesus, Our Life, I dwell in you.

*To listen to "Where We'll Never Grow Old" and "Down by the*

# *Tuesday, March 24*

## Fifth Week of Lent

Gonna lay down my sword and shield, down by the riverside.

The repetition and rhythm in this African American spiritual convey a joyful longing—this is good traveling music. The lyrics take us "down by the riverside," a place of life and freedom. In our Christian tradition, the river also symbolizes Baptism, cleansing, and renewal.

We've been traveling with and praying for those who will be initiated into the Christian life when they are baptized at the Easter Vigil. The journey of these catechumens to the "riverside" reminds us of the new identity that we all receive through the Sacrament of Baptism. Being conformed to Christ in Baptism allows us to live distinctively, bringing Christlike expectations and imagination to our communities. The world often urges us to pick up the sword and shield, but by the riverside—through the waters of Baptism where we commit to life in Christ—we lay them back down.

### *Prayer for the Morning*

Jesus, Our Living Water, through our Baptism, our lives take on the pattern of your life, Death, and Resurrection. Grant me courage to joyfully embrace this identity in a world that seems indifferent to your Gospel. Jesus, Our Way, bring me newness of life.

### *Ponder for the Day*

How has my Baptism and our Catholic community shaped my life?

### *Prayer for the Evening*

Jesus, Our Living Water, you bring us good news of the Father's mercy. Help me remain faithful to the promises of my Baptism and to find support in others who seek to live in your love. Jesus, Our Way, hold me fast.

*Riverside," scan the QR code or visit www.avemariapress.com/pages/what-wondrous-love-music.*

# *Wednesday, March 25*

## Fifth Week of Lent

I ain't gonna study war no more,
ain't gonna study war no more.

Today's spiritual dates to before the Civil War but was revived as a protest song during the Vietnam War. The music conveys a firm but joyful conviction that Christ will reign in the end. Drawn from the book of Isaiah, the lyrics articulate a powerful longing for a Savior who "shall judge between the nations, and set terms for many peoples. They shall beat their swords into plowshares and their spears into pruning hooks" (Is 2:4).

Christ comes to bring peace, a peace that we are to help create upon the earth. Our Baptism molds our lives to his and marks us indelibly with his selfless love. This is a love that drives us to care for those in need, fight for justice, and bring peace. As we prepare to renew our baptismal promises this Easter, we commit ourselves to doing his work in this world.

### *Prayer for the Morning*

Jesus, Our Joy, you established God's reign here on earth and call us to further this kingdom of truth and love. Grant me clarity to see the corners of the world where I can carry your compassion. Christ, Our Peace, lead me.

### *Ponder for the Day*

What part of my life needs more peace? And how can I lay down any weapons of discord that I might be carrying?

### *Prayer for the Evening*

Jesus, Our Joy, your coming changed our horizon and made us adopted children of an infinitely generous God. Transform the parts of me that are too small for your love. Christ, Our Peace, enlarge my heart.

*To listen to "Down by the Riverside" and "O Come, Angel Band," scan*

# Thursday, March 26

## Fifth Week of Lent

My latest sun is sinking fast,
my race is nearly run.

Lazarus, Martha, and Mary were in their routine of ordinary life when Lazarus got sick. Illness came upon him as a surprise: One day he was helping with the usual household tasks; the next he was sick in bed—and he just kept getting sicker. Had they known he would be sick, and had they known he would die, they would have planned to have Jesus nearby during that crisis. Instead, they had to send for him to come, and to come quickly.

We don't know the hour or manner of our death, but it will come for us as it did for Lazarus. Lent reminds us that we must bring urgency to the task of conversion—but there's no need to fear. The one thing we can count on that is more certain than death is Jesus's life-giving love for each one of us.

### Prayer for the Morning

Jesus, Son of the Living God, you wept at Lazarus's death, and you revealed your saving power by calling him out of his tomb. Increase my confidence in your care for me and help me to change my life to more closely imitate you. Lord of Life, I trust in you.

### Ponder for the Day

What plans can I make now to bring urgency and focus to my observance of Holy Week next week?

### Prayer for the Evening

Jesus, Son of the Living God, you came to bring us abundant life. Strengthen me to carry my crosses with courage and faithfulness so that I can follow you into new life. Lord of Life, I hope in you.

*the QR code or visit www.avemariapress.com/pages/what-wondrous-love-music.*

# *Friday, March 27*

## Fifth Week of Lent

O come, angel band,
come and around me stand.

The song we are praying with reminds us that we are accompanied through life by angels who watch over us, especially in moments of crisis and great need. In addition to the Communion of Saints who intercede for us, God sends messengers to guide us. As St. Basil the Great wrote, "Beside each believer stands an angel as protector and shepherd leading them to life."

It has been a long season, and it can be tempting to look back over the past five weeks and see all the ways we've not lived up to our hopes for Lent. But the fight isn't over! We have every spiritual advantage in our search for holiness this Lenten season: The saints and angels are with us. Let us call on them and rely on their help!

### *Prayer for the Morning*

All you saints and angels, you convey the Father's messages and lead us to life. Help me remember that what I do here on earth has eternal consequences. All in the heavenly host, be at my side this day.

### *Ponder for the Day*

During what part of this day will I likely need assistance from the heavenly helpers God sends to me?

### *Prayer for the Evening*

All you Saints and Angels, you have been walking with me every day of Lent. In this final week, lead me to greater faithfulness so that I may wholeheartedly join the feast of Easter. All in the Heavenly Host, light my way.

*To listen to "O Come, Angel Band," scan the QR code or visit*

# *Saturday, March 28*

## Fifth Week of Lent

O bear my longing heart to him who bled and died for me;
whose love now covers all my sin, and gives me victory.

Tomorrow is Palm Sunday, when we recall Jesus's triumphant entry into Jerusalem. Our celebration of Mass today takes a sharp turn into the story of the betrayal, humiliation, Crucifixion, and Death of Jesus. So begins the final days of our Lenten journey, and we must be ready to walk with Jesus every step if we want to know the transformative power of his Resurrection.

During Holy Week, we enter Jesus's agony and suffering to join the sacrifice of our own lives to his. To fully celebrate the mystery of our salvation requires vulnerability—we must be willing to *suffer with* Jesus, allowing our hearts to be pierced. This is a story of victory, but it comes at great cost.

### *Prayer for the Morning*

Jesus, Lamb of God, your suffering, Death, and Resurrection defeated everything that could stand in the way of God's love for us—even death. Soften my heart and help me turn away from the habits that diminish my ability to love as you do. Holy Redeemer, cover my sin.

### *Ponder for the Day*

How can I get ready to follow Jesus to the Cross, through the cold tomb, and into the light of Easter?

### *Prayer for the Evening*

Jesus, Lamb of God, you bled and died to bring us eternal life. As I follow you to the Cross, fortify me to bring all of myself to the mystery of your love. Holy Redeemer, give me victory.

*www.avemariapress.com/pages/what-wondrous-love-music.*

# *Sunday, March 29*

## Palm Sunday of the Passion of the Lord

Awake, my soul, and sing of him who died for thee,
and hail him as thy matchless king through all eternity.

Our Lenten practices over the past month have built up to this week. It is time to draw together the energy we've dedicated to this season and focus it on these final steps. Even if Lent has been an uneven journey, this is a day to gather our courage and resolute hearts to face what lies ahead. We stand with Jesus at the gates of Jerusalem, ready.

The crowds of today's Palm Sunday gospel acclaim Jesus as Messiah, and with them we hail him as the Anointed One come to set us free—only we know something they don't: He is a king who will wear a crown of thorns and will be lifted up on a cross, not a throne. So, we enter the enthusiasm of this day with apprehensive solemnity. For all our devotion, we, too, likely stand in this crowd with fickle hearts, only partially comprehending what the coming days will ask of us.

### *Prayer for the Morning*

Eternal King, we hail you today as our hoped-for Savior. Grant me a generous and resolute heart so that I can follow you to the Cross with a willingness to lay down my life. Messiah, reign in me.

### *Ponder for the Day*

What part of my life do I most need to bring to the Lord this Holy Week?

### *Prayer for the Evening*

Eternal King, the crowds hailed your entry into Jerusalem but could not imagine the sacrifice that lay ahead. Expand my imagination for the ways I might sacrificially love as you did. Messiah, love through me.

*To listen to "Crown Him with Many Crowns," scan the QR code or*

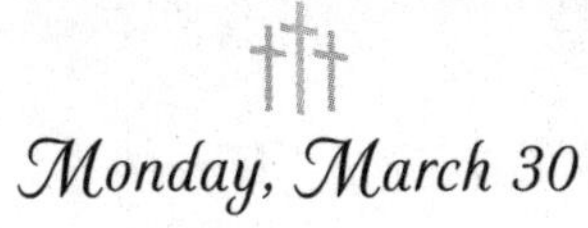

# *Monday, March 30*

## Holy Week

Crown him the Lord of love; behold his hands and side,
rich wounds, yet visible above, in beauty glorified.

This week, we will indeed crown Jesus as the Lord of love—but we will do so with a crown of thorns, which he accepts without resistance. We can behold the wounds we inflict on his pierced hands and side as "rich" and "beautiful," as our hymn for yesterday and today tells us, because of what his Death has won for us. In dying for us, Jesus made the greatest evil a source of the greatest good and opened a way for us to follow him through suffering and death to newness of life. When we follow him to the Cross, we can behold our own wounds as beautiful openings for union with our Savior, who can transform them into something good.

### *Prayer for the Morning*

Beautiful Redeemer, your love is strong and vulnerable enough to accept the worst we can do. Make my heart as tender and trusting as yours. Lord of Love, I behold your wounds with sorrow and gratitude.

### *Ponder for the Day*

What are the wounds I carry that might allow me to identify with the crucified Lord?

### *Prayer for the Evening*

Beautiful Redeemer, in dying you bring us new life. Send your Spirit of truth so that I may see with honesty both my faults and your eternal love. Lord of Love, behold my wounds and make me whole.

*visit www.avemariapress.com/pages/what-wondrous-love-music.*

# *Tuesday, March 31*

## HOLY WEEK

What a friend we have in Jesus,
all our sins and griefs to bear!

The author of this song, Joseph Scriven, certainly bore his share of grief. He was born to a wealthy family in Ireland in 1819 and, after graduating from college, was engaged to be married, but his fiancée drowned the night before the wedding. A year later, he followed a calling to serve the faithful in Canada. There, he fell in love again, but his second fiancée died from pneumonia.

When he received word that his mother was gravely ill, he wrote her a poem called "Pray Without Ceasing" to lift her spirits. He had no idea that his words would be published in newspapers and set to music and sung by millions of Christians around the world in the following two centuries. Scriven could have simply written his mother an encouraging letter, but he invested the effort to craft an inspiring poem to help her turn her suffering into prayer. His words continue to lift our hearts today.

### *Prayer for the Morning*

Loving Lord, you came to share life with us. Give me confidence that the details of my life—my joys and pains—are not too trivial for your love. Jesus, My Friend, I share my life with you.

### *Ponder for the Day*

How has Jesus been a friend to me in this Lenten journey?

### *Prayer for the Evening*

Loving Lord, you are the inexhaustible love of the Father. Thank you for your tender concern and care for me. Jesus, Our Friend, I love you.

*To listen to "What a Friend We Have in Jesus," scan the QR code or*

# *Wednesday, April 1*

## Holy Week

Jesus knows our every weakness;
take it to the Lord in prayer!

We've spent the last six weeks in prayer. If we've learned one thing from walking with the Lord through this Lent, it's that he is closer to us than we can imagine. Wherever we look for him in our experience and interior life, we find him already there, ready for us to discover that he loves us more than we know.

We have nothing to fear in placing our lives in his hands. Any guilt or shame we feel might be a rightly ordered response to the ways we've turned away from him, but those feelings do not need to get in the way of our turning back to him. He knows us through and through. He has seen both our hidden faithfulness and our shallow selfishness, and still he loves us through and through. He waits for us when we turn to him in prayer, ready to embrace us and lead us into deeper intimacy.

### *Prayer for the Morning*

Jesus, God-with-us, you reveal to us that the way to the Father is through selfless love. Help me live with your generosity and compassion. Jesus, Our Brother, pour your love into me.

### *Ponder for the Day*

What have I learned this Lent about carrying intimacy with the Lord through the rest of my day?

### *Prayer for the Evening*

Jesus, God-with-us, you wait for our return to you with open arms and a heart that never fails to give. Grow my desire for your love and let me be transformed by it. Jesus, Our Brother, I pour myself out in you.

*visit www.avemariapress.com/pages/what-wondrous-love-music.*

# *April 2*

## Holy Thursday

We believe him near.

On Holy Thursday evening, we listen to the gospel story of Jesus and his disciples at the Last Supper. In our churches, we experience the Washing of Feet as we recall how Jesus communicated his love not only for his disciples but also for us. In this sacred meal, we remember and receive anew the gift of this love, which he gives to us in his very Body and Blood through the forms of bread and wine.

In this holy remembering of what Jesus did and said, we encounter him anew. Faith allows us to receive Christ Jesus as he speaks through the words of scripture and gives himself to us through broken bread and poured wine. When we extend ourselves in service, we encounter Christ present in the least among us. We repeat the words and actions he left us this day because these are the ways we believe he is near.

### *Prayer for the Morning*

Eucharistic Lord, you meet us face-to-face when we put into action the love you share with us. Give me courage and generosity to reach out to those in need of your care. Bread of Life, help me nourish others.

### *Ponder for the Day*

How has Jesus's presence become real to me these past weeks—and how can I continue to encounter him through the Easter season?

### *Prayer for the Evening*

Eucharistic Lord, after the Last Supper, you asked your friends to watch and pray with you as you prepared to enter your Passion. May my prayer this night deepen my love for you. Bread of Life, I will follow you.

*To listen to "We Walk by Faith" and "What Wondrous Love Is This,"*

# April 3

## Good Friday

What wondrous love is this, that caused the Lord of bliss
to bear the dreadful curse for my soul.

God sent his Son to share everything about our lives: our joys, dreams, friendships, and delights, as well as our humiliation, abandonment, suffering, and death. Jesus did not deserve to experience pain and death, but he willingly embraced it out of love for us and a desire to embrace everything in the human condition. In doing so, he reveals to us what love is: a self-emptying gift. If we accept the totality of his love—how he gave everything for us—and make his wondrous love the pattern of our own lives, we will find hope.

Today, we stand with Christ at the foot of the Cross, sorrowful and grateful for his sacrifice, and willing to lay down our lives with him in order to follow his way.

### *Prayer for the Morning*

Jesus, Son of God, you carried the Cross with loving arms and gave your life away before uncomprehending strangers. Help me contemplate today the wondrous magnitude of your love. Jesus, Suffering Servant, grow and deepen my love.

### *Ponder for the Day*

In what ways can I mark today with solemnity and grateful prayer?

### *Prayer for the Evening*

Jesus, Son of God, you did not deserve the pain and death we inflicted on you, but you accepted it in love to free us from the darkness of our own worst sin and sorrow. Help me remember that you will reach across any distance to bring me to you. Jesus, Suffering Servant, deepen my hope.

*scan the QR code or visit www.avemariapress.com/pages/what-wondrous-love-music.*

# *April 4*

## Holy Saturday

Steal away, steal away home.
I ain't got long to stay here.

Today is a day of solemn silence as we recall the burial of Jesus's body and the grief of his friends and mother. Today, in memory, we join them at his tomb. Yet we know the promise of his Resurrection, so our waiting is marked by patient hope. And we keep vigil long into the night.

Our song today is an African American spiritual that contained hidden codes to help enslaved people escape Southern plantations on the Underground Railroad. It is a hymn of longing for our heavenly home—a song intended for those traveling and waiting for freedom. The ponderous and subdued music matches well the tone of our prayer today.

### *Prayer for the Morning*

Jesus, Firstborn of Creation, you taught us that a grain of wheat must fall to the earth and die in order to bear much fruit. Grant me patience and courage to anticipate the surprising ways the Father brings us life. Hope of Our Salvation, I wait for your love.

### *Ponder for the Day*

How can I build into my day today some time for intentional, solemn silence?

### *Prayer for the Evening*

Jesus, Firstborn of Creation, you died to set us free. Thank you for this blessed season of Lent; help me rejoice in the gifts you bring. Hope of Our Salvation, I trust in your love.

*To listen to "Steal Away" and "I Know That My Redeemer Lives," scan*

# April 5

## Easter Sunday

I know that my Redeemer lives; what comfort this sweet sentence gives!
He lives, he lives, who once was dead; he lives, my everlasting Head.

Christ Jesus, the one who was abandoned, tortured, and killed, will not accept the distance we try to place between himself and us. Christ has taken our rejection and returned it with a wondrous love, drawing us ever closer to himself. The Father raised him up that first Easter, which opened the gates of heaven for all eternity. Christ is there to meet us in our daily experience whenever we turn to him with vulnerable hearts, ready to embrace his truth and everlasting love.

Christ's Resurrection proves that nothing can stand in the way of the new life the Father intends for us. Because of the wondrous love of the Resurrection, Jesus has become a font of eternal life for us—he is the source of unity between believers and a means of union with the Father. Christ, our risen Lord, has given us a new identity and a new destiny.

### *Prayer for the Morning*

Jesus, Dayspring, with total trust in the Father, you loved us to the end, and the Father raised you from the dead. Help me love you to the end and trust that you will bring me to eternal life with you. Risen Lord, lead me.

### *Ponder for the Day*

What fruit from Lent do I want to carry through this Easter season?

### *Prayer for the Evening*

Jesus, Dayspring, because you emptied yourself, the Father exalted you and gave you a name that is above every other name. Remain with me at the center of my life so that I may follow you to the Father. Risen Lord, I praise you.

*the QR code or visit www.avemariapress.com/pages/what-wondrous-love-music.*

# Complete Lyrics

## Week of Ash Wednesday

*Wednesday, February 18-Saturday, February 21*

### Take Up Your Cross

*Author: Charles W. Everest*

Take up your cross, the Savior said,
if you would my disciple be;
deny yourself, the world forsake,
and humbly follow after me.

Take up your cross, be not ashamed!
Let not disgrace your spirit fill!
For God himself endured to die
upon a cross, on Calvary's hill.

Take up your cross, which gives you strength,
which makes your trembling spirit brave:
'Twill guide you to a better home
and lead to vict'ry o'er the grave.

Take up your cross, and follow Christ,
nor think till death to lay it down;
for only they who bear the cross
may hope to wear the glorious crown.

## First Week of Lent

*Sunday, February 22-Saturday, February 28*

### Forty Days and Forty Nights

*Author: George Hunt Smyttan*

Forty days and forty nights you were fasting in the wild;
forty days and forty nights tempted, and yet undefiled.

Sunbeams scorching all the day; chilly dew-drops nightly shed;
prowling beasts about your way; stones your pillow; earth your bed.

Shall not we your sorrow share, and from earthly joys abstain,
fasting with unceasing prayer, glad with you to suffer pain?

And if Satan, vexing sore, flesh or spirit should assail,
Christ, his vanquisher before, grant we may not faint or fail.

So shall we have peace divine; holier gladness ours be due;
round us, too, shall angels shine, such as ministered to you.

Keep, oh, keep us, Savior dear, ever constant at your side;
that we may with you appear in your resurrection-tide.

## Wayfaring Stranger

*American folk song*

I'm just a poor wayfaring stranger, I'm trav'ling through this world below;
there is no sickness, toil, nor danger, in that bright land to which I go.

I'm going there to see my father, I'm going there no more to roam;
I'm just a going over Jordan, I'm just a going over home.

I know dark clouds will gather o'er me, I know my pathway's rough and steep;
but golden fields lie out before me, where weary eyes no more shall weep.

I'm going there to see my mother, she said she'd meet me when I come;
I'm just a going over Jordan, I'm just a going over home.

I want to sing salvation's story, in concert with the blood-washed band;
I want to wear a crown of glory, when I get home to that good land.

I'm going there to see my loved ones, they passed before me one by one;
I'm just a going over Jordan, I'm just a going over home.

I'll soon be free from every trial, this form will rest beneath the sod;
I'll drop the cross of self-denial, and enter in my home with God.

I'm going there to see my Savior, who shed for me his precious blood;
I'm just a going over Jordan, I'm just a going over home.

## Second Week of Lent

### *Sunday, March 1-Saturday, March 7*

### Beautiful Savior

*Translator: Joseph Augustus Seiss*

Beautiful Savior, King of Creation, Son of God and Son of Man!
Truly I'd love thee, truly I'd serve thee, Light of My Soul, My Joy, My Crown.

Fair are the meadows, fair are the woodlands, robed in flow'rs of blooming spring;
Jesus is fairer, Jesus is purer; he makes our sorr'wing spirit sing.

Fair is the sunshine, fair is the moonlight, bright the sparkling stars on high;
Jesus shines brighter, Jesus shines purer than all the angels in the sky.

Beautiful Savior, Lord of the Nations, Son of God and Son of Man!
Glory and honor, praise, adoration, now and forevermore be thine!

### Blessed Assurance

*Author: Fanny Crosby*

Blessed assurance, Jesus is mine!
Oh, what a foretaste of glory divine!
Heir of Salvation, Purchase of God,
born of his Spirit, washed in his blood.

*Refrain:*
This is my story, this is my song,
praising my Savior all the day long.
This is my story, this is my song,
praising my Savior all the day long.

Perfect communion, perfect delight,
visions of rapture now burst on my sight.
Angels descending bring from above
echoes of mercy, whispers of love. *Refrain*

Perfect submission, all is at rest.
I in my Savior am happy and bless'd,
watching and waiting, looking above,
filled with his goodness, lost in his love. *Refrain*

# Third Week of Lent

## *Sunday, March 8-Saturday, March 14*

## Softly and Tenderly Jesus Is Calling

*Author: Will L. Thompson*

Softly and tenderly Jesus is calling, calling for you and for me;
see, on the portals he's waiting and watching, watching for you and for me.

*Refrain:*
Come home, come home; you who are weary come home;
earnestly, tenderly, Jesus is calling, calling, O sinner, come home!

Why should we tarry when Jesus is pleading, pleading for you and for me?
Why should we linger and heed not his mercies, mercies for you and for me?
*Refrain*

Time is now fleeting, the moments are passing, passing from you and from me;
shadows are gathering, deathbeds are coming, coming for you and for me.
*Refrain*

O for the wonderful love he has promised, promised for you and for me!
Though we have sinned, he has mercy and pardon, pardon for you and for me.
*Refrain*

## There's a Wideness in God's Mercy

*Author: Frederick William Faber*

There's a wideness in God's mercy, like the wideness of the sea.
There's a kindness in God's justice, which is more than liberty.

There is welcome for the sinner, and more graces for the good.
There is mercy with the Savior, there is healing in his blood.

But we make God's love too narrow by false limits of our own,
and we magnify its strictness with a zeal God will not own.

For the love of God is broader than the measures of the mind,
and the heart of the Eternal is most wonderfully kind.

If our love were but more simple, we should rest upon God's word,
and our lives would be illumined by the presence of our Lord.

# Fourth Week of Lent

## *Sunday, March 15-Saturday, March 21*

## On Jordan's Stormy Banks I Stand

*Author: Samuel Stennett*

On Jordan's stormy banks I stand, and cast a wishful eye
to Canaan's fair and happy land, where my possessions lie.

*Refrain:*
I am bound for the promised land, I am bound for the promised land;
oh, who will come and go with me? I am bound for the promised land.

O'er all those wide extended plains shines one eternal day;
there God the Son forever reigns, and scatters night away. *Refrain*

No chilling winds or poisonous breath can reach that healthful shore;
sickness and sorrow, pain and death, are felt and feared no more. *Refrain*

When I shall reach that happy place, I'll be forever blest,
for I shall see my Father's face, and in his bosom rest. *Refrain*

## Christ Be Near at Either Hand

*Traditional Irish text (The Lorica of St. Patrick)*

Christ be near at either hand, Christ behind, before me stand;
Christ with me where'er I go, Christ around, above, below.

Christ be in my heart and mind, Christ within my soul enshrined;
Christ control my wayward heart; Christ abide and ne'er depart.

Christ my life and only way, Christ my lantern night and day;
Christ be my unchanging friend, guide and shepherd to the end.

## The King of Love My Shepherd Is

*Author: H. W. Baker*

The King of Love my shepherd is, whose goodness fails me never.
I nothing lack if I am his, and he is mine forever.

Where streams of living water flow, my ransomed soul he leadeth;
and where the verdant pastures grow, with food celestial feedeth.

Perverse and foolish, oft I strayed, but yet in love he sought me;
and on his shoulder gently laid, and home, rejoicing, brought me.

In death's dark vale I fear no ill, with thee, dear Lord, beside me;
thy rod and staff my comfort still, thy cross before to guide me.

Thou spreadst a table in my sight; thy unction grace bestoweth;
and oh, what transport of delight from thy pure chalice floweth!

And so through all the length of days, thy goodness faileth never;
Good Shepherd, may I sing thy praise within thy house forever.

## Fifth Week of Lent

*Sunday, March 22-Saturday, March 28*

### Where We'll Never Grow Old

*Author: James C. Moore (1914)*

I have heard of a land on the faraway strand,
'tis a beautiful home of the soul; built by Jesus on high,
there we never shall die, 'tis a land where we never grow old.

*Refrain:*
Never grow old, where we'll never grow old,
in a land where we'll never grow old; never grow old,
where we'll never grow old, in a land where we'll never grow old.

In that beautiful home where we'll nevermore roam,
we shall be in the sweet by and by; happy praise to the King
through eternity sing, 'tis a land where we never shall die. *Refrain*

When our work here is done and the life crown is won,
and our troubles and trials are o'er, all our sorrows will end,
and our voices will blend with the loved ones who've gone on before. *Refrain*

### Down by the Riverside

*African American spiritual*

Gonna lay down my sword and shield,
down by the riverside,

down by the riverside,
down by the riverside;
gonna lay down my sword and shield,
down by the riverside,
down by the riverside.
I ain't gonna study war no more.
Ain't gonna study war no more,
ain't gonna study war no more,
I ain't gonna study war no more,
ain't gonna study war no more,
ain't gonna study war no more.

Gonna lay down my burden,
down by the riverside,
down by the riverside,
down by the riverside;
gonna lay down my burden,
down by the riverside,
down by the riverside.
I ain't gonna study war no more.
Ain't gonna study war no more,
ain't gonna study war no more,
I ain't gonna study war no more,
ain't gonna study war no more,
ain't gonna study war no more.

## O Come, Angel Band

*Author: Jefferson Hascall*

My latest sun is sinking fast, my race is nearly run;
my strongest trials now are past, my triumph is begun.

*Refrain:*
O come, angel band, come and around me stand;
O bear me away on your snowy wings to my immortal home.
O bear me away on your snowy wings to my immortal home.

I know I'm near the holy ranks of friends and kindred dear;
I hear the waves on Jordan's banks, the crossing must be near. *Refrain*

I've almost reached my heav'nly home, my spirit loudly sings;
your holy ones, behold, they come! I hear the noise of wings. *Refrain*

O bear my longing heart to him who bled and died for me;
whose love now covers all my sin, and gives me victory. *Refrain*

## Holy Week

### *Palm Sunday, March 29–Holy Saturday, April 4*

### Crown Him with Many Crowns

*Author: Matthew Bridges | Alterer: Godfrey Thring*

Crown him with many crowns, the Lamb upon his throne.
Hark! how the heavenly anthem drowns all music but its own.
Awake, my soul, and sing of him who died for thee,
and hail him as thy matchless king through all eternity.

Crown him the Lord of life, who triumphed o'er the grave,
and rose victorious in the strife for those he came to save;
his glories now we sing who died and rose on high,
who died eternal life to bring, and lives that death may die.

Crown him the Lord of love; behold his hands and side,
rich wounds, yet visible above, in beauty glorified;
no angels in the sky can fully bear that sight,
but downward bends their burning eye at mysteries so bright.

Crown him the Lord of years, the potentate of time,
creator of the rolling spheres, ineffably sublime.
All hail, Redeemer, hail! for thou hast died for me;
thy praise shall never, never fail throughout eternity.

### What a Friend We Have in Jesus

*Author: Joseph Medlicott Scriven*

What a friend we have in Jesus, all our sins and griefs to bear!
What a privilege to carry everything to God in prayer!
O what peace we often forfeit, O what needless pain we bear,
all because we do not carry everything to God in prayer!

Have we trials and temptations? Is there trouble anywhere?
We should never be discouraged; take it to the Lord in prayer!
Can we find a friend so faithful who will all our sorrows share?
Jesus knows our every weakness; take it to the Lord in prayer!

Are we weak and heavy laden, cumbered with a load of care?
Precious Savior, still our refuge—take it to the Lord in prayer!
Do your friends despise, forsake you? Take it to the Lord in prayer!
In his arms he'll take and shield you; you will find a solace there.

## We Walk by Faith

*Author: Henry Alford*

We walk by faith, and not by sight; no gracious words we hear
from him who spoke as none ne'er spoke, but we believe him near.

We may not touch his hands and side, nor follow where he trod;
but in his promise we rejoice, and cry, "My Lord and God!"

Help then, O Lord, our unbelief; and may our faith abound,
to call on you when you are near, and seek where you are found.

That when our lives of faith are done, in realms of clearer light,
we may behold you as you are, with full and endless sight.

## What Wondrous Love Is This

*Author: Anonymous*

What wondrous love is this, O my soul, O my soul!
What wondrous love is this, O my soul!
What wondrous love is this, that caused the Lord of bliss
to bear the dreadful curse for my soul, for my soul,
to bear the dreadful curse for my soul.

When I was sinking down, sinking down, sinking down,
when I was sinking down, O my soul!
When I was sinking down beneath God's righteous frown,
Christ laid aside his crown for my soul, for my soul,
Christ laid aside his crown for my soul.

To God and to the Lamb I will sing, I will sing;

to God and to the Lamb, I will sing.
To God and to the Lamb who is the great "I AM,"
while millions join the theme, I will sing, I will sing,
while millions join the theme, I will sing.

## Steal Away

*African American spiritual*

*Refrain:*
Steal away, steal away, steal away to Jesus.
Steal away, steal away home. I ain't got long to stay here.

My Lord, he calls me, he calls me by the thunder;
the trumpet sounds within my soul; I ain't got long to stay here. *Refrain*

Green trees are bending, poor sinners stand a-trembling;
the trumpet sounds within my soul; I ain't got long to stay here. *Refrain*

My Lord, he calls me, he calls me by the lightning;
the trumpet sounds within my soul; I ain't got long to stay here. *Refrain*

Tombstones are bursting, poor sinners are a-trembling;
the trumpet sounds within my soul; I ain't got long to stay here. *Refrain*

# Easter Sunday

*April 5*

## I Know That My Redeemer Lives

*Author: Samuel Medley*

I know that my Redeemer lives; what comfort this sweet sentence gives!
He lives, he lives, who once was dead; he lives, my everlasting Head.

He lives triumphant from the grave, he lives eternally to save,
he lives all-glorious in the sky, he lives exalted there on high.

He lives to bless me with his love, he lives to plead for me above,
he lives my hungry soul to feed, he lives to help in time of need.

He lives to grant me rich supply, he lives to guide me with his eye,
he lives to comfort me when faint, he lives to hear my soul's complaint.

He lives to silence all my fears, he lives to wipe away my tears,
he lives to calm my troubled heart, he lives all blessings to impart.

He lives, my kind, wise, heav'nly Friend, he lives and loves me to the end;
he lives, and while he lives, I'll sing; he lives, my Prophet, Priest, and King.

He lives and grants me daily breath; he lives and I shall conquer death;
he lives my mansion to prepare; he lives to bring me safely there.

He lives, all glory to his name! He lives, my Jesus, still the same.
Oh, the sweet joy this sentence gives, "I know that my Redeemer lives!"

Founded in 1865 by Fr. Edward Sorin, CSC, **Ave Maria Press** is an apostolate of the Congregation of Holy Cross, United States Province of Priests and Brothers. Ave is a nonprofit Catholic publishing ministry that serves the spiritual and formative needs of the Church and its schools, institutions, and ministers; Christian individuals and families; and others seeking spiritual nourishment.

Ave remains one of the oldest continually operating Catholic publishing houses in the country and a leader in publishing Catholic high school religion textbooks, ministry resources, and books on prayer and spirituality.

In the tradition of Holy Cross, Ave is committed, as an educator in the faith, to help people know, love, and serve God and to spread the gospel of Jesus Christ through books and other resources.

Ave Maria Press perpetuates Fr. Sorin's vision to honor Mary and provide an important outlet for good Catholic writing.

**Josh Noem** is the editorial director at Ave Maria Press. He began his writing career as a Catholic journalist and served as editor of the FaithND and Grotto Network platforms before joining Ave in 2022. His book *The End of Ending* was recognized as one of the best Catholic novels of 2021.

Noem grew up in the Black Hills of South Dakota and earned a master of divinity degree from the University of Notre Dame.

Noem and his family live in South Bend, Indiana. Find more of his writing at joshnoem.substack.com.

Website: joshnoem.substack.com
Instagram: @josh.noem